God is Love

The Heart of All Creation

—

THOMAS KEATING

in Conversation with Carl Arico

WAYFARER BOOKS
SAN JUAN MOUNTAINS, COLORADO

WAYFARER BOOKS
SAN JUAN MOUNTAINS, COLORADO

SUPPORTING INDIGENOUS FUTURES
1% GIVEN BACK

WORKS BY THOMAS KEATING

Open Mind, Open Heart

God Is All In All

Heartfulness

That We May Be One

Intimacy with God

Journey to the Center

Reawakenings

Spirituality, Contemplation & Transformation

The Daily Reader for Contemplative Living

The Thomas Keating Reader

The Mystery of Christ

FOREWORD

Recently I asked my class, "What is love?" Twenty-five undergraduates looked at me quizzically, as if I had just asked them to solve the equation for the Higgs boson. Not one person could provide an adequate answer. However, when I asked, "Have you ever experienced love?" they unanimously answered "yes." We know love through experience, but defining love leaves us speechless. No word can adequately capture the meaning of "love," for its essence is clothed in the relationships it engenders.

The Bible verse "God is love" from 1 John 4:8 encapsulates one of Christianity's most profound theological concepts. This passage suggests that love isn't merely something God does or feels—it is fundamental to God's very nature and essence. Love is God's defining attribute. Unlike other qualities that God possesses, love is God's very being. All God's actions and attributes flow from this core identity. Love is relational, unitive, and creative. The Trinity symbolizes the intrinsic nature of God as love: infinite potential, ultimately expressed, dynamically ecstatic. God is not creative because God decides to be so; God is creative because God is love. Love goes forth in the name of God and empowers life to respond in love with a resounding "yes." This "yes" to divine love is the dynamism of the Big Bang, the stars and galaxies, the formation of planets and earthly life, and ultimately a self-conscious being who can respond to love as a radically free decision. For love to stay true to its essence, it must perpetually grow. The divine dynamism of love drives reality forward, moving it toward ever-new relationships of love with a divine goal forever beyond our full grasp. Life and love are cumulative, developing in ways that are always new and always more. Love can never remain static, as Jesuit priest and scientist Pierre Teilhard de Chardin realized. Love is the core energy of the universe. God is the name of divine love's longing for more life. As love grows, God's existence is brought into explicit awareness. God is the center of love in which all differences are resolved in the beauty of the whole.

If God is love, then openness is the fundamental law of God. Out of love comes a world containing creatures endowed with the capacity to love. God seeks a personal relationship with creatures; God is intensely interested in and genuinely affected by their actions and decisions. God is not the "unmoved Mover" of Aristotle but "the most moved Mover," as described by rabbi and theologian Abraham Joshua Heschel. God enjoys a highly interactive relation to the world wherein God's creatures have significant freedom, a world unfolding in novelty and creativity. Out of love and because of love, God is open to the world and the world is open to God. If God is love, then God can do no other than be affected by the world. As the Cappadocian Fathers realized, "God's ultimate reality cannot be located in substance (what it is in itself) but only in personhood: what God is toward another. Only in communion can God be what God is, and only in communion can God be at all."

If God can do no other than love, then God's omnipotence is God's capacity to love with all its costs, including loving all who reject or denounce God. God's love is God's freedom to be who God is. Since love causes God to be, God cannot not love. God's commitment to creaturely welfare remains unconditional. Coercion has no place in love; thus, our response to God is a choice for love which means, creatures are self-determining—God is not responsible for everything that happens in the world. We are the cause of our own sin or brokenness and bear the responsibility for our own actions. For God to exist, love must be actualized.

In his essay on human energy, Teilhard de Chardin wrote: "Driven by the forces of love, the fragments of the world seek each other so that the world may come to being." He felt that nothing less than an energy of centration, radically distinct from but integral to matter, could ultimately explain evolution. He called this dynamic energy of attraction "Omega," an energy of love that exists within all things yet not subject to the death of all things—a dynamic presence of love that resists entropy and undergirds evolution. Omega is God. Teilhard's concept of Omega represents both the transcendent goal and the immanent driving force of evolution. As the ultimate point of cosmic convergence, Omega is simultaneously the end toward which evolution moves and the energy that propels it forward. This dual nature of Omega—transcendent yet intimately present—resolves the apparent tension between the ineffable mystery of divine love and God's involvement in the world. Since love causes God to be who God is, every act of love is an act of God's presence, and every act of God's presence is an act of transcendence. God is the name of love that transcends the world precisely by drawing it toward ultimate fulfillment through love's irresistible attraction. In Teilhard's view, God becomes God only up ahead, in the final resolution of life, the completion of all in love.

Teilhard's vision offers profound implications for understanding human purpose and responsibility. If we exist within an unfinished universe still moving toward its fulfillment in Omega, then human activity becomes integral to the cosmos achieving its destiny. Our creative endeavors, scientific discoveries, social structures, and spiritual aspirations all participate in the cosmos's movement toward greater unity and complexity. Far from being passive spectators, humans are active co-creators with God, responsible for advancing the evolutionary process through conscious choices that increase love and unity.

This co-creative relationship transforms our understanding of spirituality as well. Rather than focusing solely on personal salvation or escape from the world, authentic spirituality involves aligning oneself with the evolutionary current moving toward greater unity. For Teilhard, the highest spiritual practice is to participate consciously in building a world of greater communion and complexity. This "divinization" of human effort gives cosmic significance to all authentic human work that contributes to unification—whether scientific, artistic, social, or political.

The insights of Father Thomas Keating on love are similar to those of Teilhard de Chardin. These two visionaries invite us to participate consciously in the ongoing creation of the world, aligning our lives with the fundamental energy of love that has driven the universe from simplicity to complexity, from unconsciousness to consciousness, from isolation to communion. Science observes this energy as the mysterious tendency toward greater complexity against the background of entropy. Faith recognizes it as love—the divine presence at the heart of an unfinished universe, drawing it toward completion.

The universe is a love story—a narrative of separation and reunion, difference and communion, in which each emergent level of complexity represents a new chapter in the cosmic romance between the yearning of God and nature's potential for more life. Humanity stands at a critical juncture in this story, capable for the first time of consciously participating in or obstructing the movement toward greater unity. Our choices matter, not just for human welfare, but for the fulfillment of the cosmic process itself. By choosing love—by acting to increase unity while preserving diversity—we align ourselves with the fundamental energy that has driven evolution from the beginning and will carry it to completion in the embrace of Omega, where all things will ultimately converge in the fullness of divine love.

—Ilia Delio

Spring 2025

INTRODUCTION

―

by Carl J. Arico

This book is an edited transcript of a DVD series that was filmed at St. Benedict's Monastery in Snowmass, Colorado in July 2013. Four days of filming. Nine hours of material.

What a joy it was to spend that time with Father Thomas–exhilarating, insightful, profound! The title of this series did not occur to us automatically. We had all sorts of discussions about what the title should be. We considered ideas such as "Evolving Consciousness," "Divine Life," "Divine Love," "Divine Presence," "The Heart of the World." Then we consulted with Father Thomas, who said, "'Divine Love'? That's just a little too contained. Why don't you just call the series 'God?'"

Well, the committee went back and looked at it and thought about it. We decided against the title "God" because we wanted to touch on the essence of God and help people connect to what the series was about. But it was a great help that Father Thomas suggested the title that he did because that led us to the current title *God is Love: The Heart of All Creation.*

Now, the topics that were covered in the nine hours of filming were vast. We talked about cosmology, human evolution, divine evolution, consciousness. We even had a wonderful session on playing with God, silence and Centering Prayer, surrendering to God's love.

We ask God to bless you and take care of you as you read, reflect, respond, and rest in the power of this gift: *God Is Love: The Heart of All Creation.*

> —Carl J. Arico
> Easter 2017

Prologue

A human being is part of the whole,
called by us 'Universe'; a part limited in time and space.
One experiences oneself ... as something separated
from the rest—a kind of optical delusion of one's
consciousness. Our task must be to free ourselves
from this prison by widening our circle
of compassion to embrace all living creatures
and the whole of nature in its beauty.

—ALBERT EINSTEIN

Father Carl: What are your thoughts on evolutionary consciousness?

Father Thomas: I think that evolutionary consciousness is extremely important. Nowadays, it needs to be placed in a context that is solidly grounded in the discoveries of modern science—and, of course, with the understanding that further developments are always possible or even likely.

In my understanding, evolution occurs on several levels: first on the material or physical level; then on the biological level; and finally on the spiritual level—and perhaps a few other levels in between or beyond. The significant book that has been helpful for beginners in learning this new cosmology and explaining how the universe actually works is Tom Berry's *The Universe Story*. After Berry's death, Brian Swimme has continued to develop Berry's remarkable research.

This evolutionary view of creation differs from what scripture presents, which was based on the cosmology that existed at that time. While much truth is contained in scriptural cosmology, it doesn't satisfy our vastly increased understanding of how the universe continues to expand and how its infinitesimal quality continues to unfold. It was only recently that scientists discovered the Higgs boson. This seems to be the principle of changing invisible energy into visible forms of one kind or another. This new science is only at its beginning, but the hypotheses are multiplying, and further experiments are being conducted.

So, in this context, we're looking at a God today who is just plain different from the one that we previously perceived. There's nothing wrong with this because God adjusts himself to our limitations. There seems to be an intent or a plan in creation to bring the manifestation of the Unknowable One into forms of relationship or evidence that awaken in us a greater capacity to love. We need to recognize something that has been traditional in Christian mystical theology and that is equally reflected in the Islamic wisdom of someone like Ibn al-Arabi and by the great Hindu pundit Shankara.

Each of these, along with Meister Eckhart, represents the epitome of the discussion about Ultimate Reality, Ultimate Mystery, or Being Beyond Being.

I won't say that what we have learned up until now is useless. It was necessary as fundamental preparation for the human condition evolving from material sources, in order to give us a chance to know and love God more. We normally love most what we know best. If our knowledge of God is severely limited by the lack of evolution beyond our rational faculties, then when these faculties start to evolve, it's wonderful news! Our love of God can now be expanded on the basis of proven facts. In this sense I think we have to look upon science as an equal voice in religious discussion because it is revealing to us things we cannot know with our ordinary senses and that can only be revealed through the technological extension of our senses that modern science has made possible.

The problem of science, of course, is that it doesn't deal with absolutes. It is only beginning to put its big toe, so to speak, into the great ocean of mystical wisdom and experience that can no longer be denied, while still respecting principles of scientific inquiry.

The purpose of this series of reflections is to try to deepen our concept of the "new God." To do this, we have to stretch our understanding of some terms and dogmas to include the vision that mystics, or those advancing into higher stages of consciousness, perceive spontaneously as they become liberated from their attachment to narrow sense and rational experience. Not that sense including rational experience isn't good—it's just never the whole story.

In my understanding, God is more and more trying to move the human family to the next stage of human consciousness, which is the capacity to receive and respond to intuitive insights rather than to rely as heavily as we do on a rational, technological, or dominating worldview in which human nature is thought of as the boss and in charge of the rest of the universe. This worldview loses the precious insight into the equality of all creatures, especially of humans, and cannot recognize the truth that there is ultimately only one Self who is God manifesting in us.

The Divine Presence is happening in, through, and amidst every detail of our life, so it should never be left out of our conscious awareness. I think that this is what is meant in Scripture by "living in the house of God." The psalmist prays that he may stay in the house of God all the days of his life—and that house is creation. If you are a part of creation, you are in its atmosphere, environment, or whatever you want to call it. In any case, the Divine Presence is always there in everything that happens, whether we pay any attention to it or not, and it is here with all its qualities that are—if we humans experience them—personal and immensely attracting, including compassion, forgiveness, caring, concern, encouragement, playfulness, experimenting, and testing.

The Divine Presence as Presence penetrates all that exists. Everyone by virtue of coming into existence is in relationship to it just by being born. Moreover, we are emerging, through the evolutionary process, into a new kind of creature. This doctrine is really important for our personal relationship with Christ because it emphasizes the divine relationship that is not only possible, but is already the fact. Christ is in relationship to every human being and everybody is in relationship to Christ right now.

ONE

Cosmology

Everything is needed. Without the perfection
of each part, something is lacking from the whole. Each
particular being in the universe is needed by the entire universe. With this understanding of our
profound kinship with all life, we can establish
the basis for a flourishing Earth community.
A vast mystery is being enacted in which we
each participate in a unique way.

—THOMAS BERRY

Let us reflect about the God of science and how profoundly scientific discoveries are affecting our theology. It is time for theology to look at those discoveries with a theological perspective and to be willing to modify in some degree, especially where the evidence is strong, the way we have thought about God up until now, especially in the area of cosmology. For instance, common scientific opinion teaches that everything in this universe that our senses observe and that our technology can uncover is, at the deepest level, revealing the infinite. It is a revelation of who God is. And it is consistent with the early Christian Church Fathers, who said there are in fact two books of revelation: one is the Bible and the other is nature.

Consider a sunset, for example. Yes, it is beautiful and lifts your spirits up—but what makes the sunset happen? Or the sunrise? And where did the sun come from? Where did it all come from? Science has given us very strong evidence supporting the hypothesis that everything in this universe comes from a super-infinitesimal pocket of energy that contained in some way all the energy that has ever been available in this universe and that is now expanding at a million miles an hour in every direction without any sign of letting up. We don't even know why it is expanding. Dark energy is believed by some scientists to be about 75% of the universe, and nobody knows what it actually is. They just know *that* it is.

The material and physical nature of evolution is beautifully described in *Journey of the Universe* by Brian Swimme and Mary Evelyn Tucker, which describes what the universe looked like a trillionth of a second after the big bang. (The mathematics of this can apparently be figured-out on a computer.) The initial blast created the first two elements—hydrogen and helium—which then began to expand at a great rate over time. Nature needs time to do its thing.

It took a few million years for the initial blast to cool off enough for other elements to appear. In the collision of different masses of material, new elements were formed, a process that required certain extreme

12

temperatures. All the elements have gradually come into being including those necessary for life such as oxygen and carbon, but they emerged millions of light years apart. Now we are talking about colossal collisions that produced materials that turned into stars and then planets, and then supernovas with gravity so great that even light cannot emerge from them. As these supernovas die, they draw into themselves everything around including light. Eventually, as they collapse, they explode all that is left of their energy into the universe in every direction. They give themselves up completely and die, you might say. If you looked into the sky over just an inch of space, you would probably be looking at billions of galaxies. Each galaxy has billions of stars. And all these galaxies are expanding into whatever was there before—but no one knows what that is!

From scientific cosmology we get an idea of creation that is, to say the least, awesome.

Creation was awesome even when it was presented in the old cosmology of Earth sitting on four pillars with an arch of a sky overhead that opened every now and then to provide rain. The new cosmology offers an

13

infinitude of forms that no human mind can grasp. For example, on the planetary level, there seems to be other planets like ours in the universe, perfectly placed around a sun, so that it is not too hot, not too cold, and not too battered by stray material from the universe.

In any case, that describes the active evolution in which the creative energy of the God that we call the Creator, brought our galaxy and this little planet to just the right place at the right time so that materials from outer space, like units of energy and living matter itself, came together and human life could eventually emerge.

The *National Geographic* recently published an article on plankton. Billions and billions of these tiny creatures, sub-sub-sub microscopic, moving out of Antarctica, affect the flow of the oceans by their underwater presence and feed the bigger fish. All these interactions of living things in relationship with Earth produce a planet that is dynamically changing on a day-to-day basis. Everything is completely connected and interrelated. This fact is both fascinating and worrisome because human ingenuity has now hastened some of the events that normally would take place in nature over thousands of years. We do not know whether nature will be able to handle the effects humans have had on it, or whether we will be willing to moderate some of our activities in relationship to damage done to the atmosphere and our ecology—as well as our relationship to other people and civilizations. What we do know is that material evolution occurred in a place where life could take root.

Life did take root, and in the course of four billion years has gradually evolved. According to biologists, this evolution is manifested by the more complex creatures that have emerged and by the interconnectedness that produces new species. It is amazing that our particular bodies have emerged from one-celled creatures that still exist and have to exist for the sake of the ecology of the planet. The evolution of life favored forms that were increasingly more complex, so that after several billion years, the higher mammals began to come into existence.

Five thousand years ago, this evolutionary development produced a human brain that could be described as "rational." Then came the Axial period, as it is sometimes called, in which in every known civilization, a further development of human thought resulted in the formation of religious inspiration and philosophical ideas.

This development took place very slowly and involved the formation of the human brain and eventually the neocortex, which allowed humans not only to become thinking animals but also to become capable of abstract thought, altruism, language, religion, and self-consciousness. The brain is unquestionably the masterpiece of creation up until now. It has been evolving, as archaeology and anthropology have proved. And there is no reason why it should not continue to evolve, unless we ourselves destroy the process.

This evolution has not been a straight path up a mountain or the direct development of human powers. Rather it has been growth and regression in times of difficulty to the instincts that God created in the lower animals such as violence, which is not an innate human trait, but is one way that our animal nature continues to work in us.

An important consideration for religious development is that the new powers of the human brain for abstract thinking, compassion, forgiveness, and relationship must also be accompanied by the pre-human brain, the animal brain, in order for us to continue to live in this world. We have to eat; we have to be nourished; we have to grow. The group has to reproduce if human evolution is to continue. Religions have tried to figure out ways to reduce the dominance of the instinctual drives inherited from our animal ancestors, but the archaeological evidence seems to show that humans slowly found their identity and were able to express it in art, and religious practices, and in relationships with others, with nature, and with Ultimate Reality.

We are dealing with the God whom we can know in some degree through creation, through grace, and through sound teaching. That knowledge always implies that we must develop practices that help human nature to heal its wounds, such as practices that are proposed by almost every religious tradition. This evolutionary healing process teaches, in effect, that creation was not a one-time event. Furthermore, it's not only continuous, but going someplace—towards a divine relationship that involves the whole human family and not just the great mystics, in a movement into the Unknowable.

The idea that this process is continuing, or maybe has just begun, is fascinating because there is no telling where it might go. The end is fairly clear in the words of the Bible which affirm that "God will be all in all." Or, in the language of St. Paul, "Christ will be everything in everyone." What does that mean?"

TWO

—

Human Evolution

Love one another. Either we must doubt the value
of everything around us, or we must utterly believe in
the possibility, and I should now add in the inevitable
consequences, of universal love. Love one another,
recognizing in the heart of each of you the same
God who is being born. Those words, first spoken two
thousand years ago, now begin to reveal themselves as
the essential structural law of what we call progress
and evolution. They enter the scientific field
of cosmic energy and its necessary laws.

— PIERRE TEILHARD DE CHARDIN

Evolution is only at the beginning of human possibilities. But such thinkers as Teilhard de Chardin, who propose evolutionary development as God's way of creating, suggests that the divine plan is moving humans with their rational level of consciousness toward a deeper kind of knowing. Aldous Huxley expresses it this way: "In humans the universe becomes conscious of itself."

Evolution does not in any way contradict the power of God to handle and guide all creation and to bring about his plan, but it does suggest that God is revealing to us how he performs this occupation and is sharing with us secrets that other creatures have not been capable of understanding or receiving. Our present time, which some anthropologists see as a possible new axial period, may move us into levels of intuitive knowledge that are more in line with the way that the invisible energies of creation actually operate.

Evolution is better understood if we take into account three ways that things can happen.

First of all, God can intervene at every step and move the evolutionary process along faster and raise up the right people to further that plan. It allows us to share as much of the divine life as our created limitations can possibly receive. In any case, God's power can intervene in any point, anywhere, any time, however visibly or invisibly. He is the God of all that is. People who are concerned that evolution will do away with God mistakenly reach that conclusion because they misunderstand the theory of evolution.

First of all then, God can intervene. Secondly, he has created various forms of life, in the plant and animal world which function by instinct, a kind of interior blueprint that they follow as a matter of course. They do the three things life is supposed to do: grow, be nourished, and contribute to the reproduction of their species. Over millions of years life keeps producing new and more complex forms as new creatures pass on their own inherited patterns to their progeny.

In this case we cannot apply our subjective perspectives to nature's more brutish expressions. When we see a lion chasing a doe, for example, we usually take the part of the doe and hope that it will get away. But, in fact, the lion has no dislike of the doe; it is just time for lunch! The lion has to eat something and the food chain is part of the evolutionary process. Animals do God's will as enshrined in their primitive level of consciousness. Human consciousness with its endowment of a certain degree of free choice involves personal awareness and self-consciousness.

Humans, who have the gift of freedom of choice, do not have freedom as such, because absolute freedom is ultimately who God is. For us, true freedom is doing what is right and true and good in every situation. Humans are invited to share in God's freedom by moderating their instinctual needs in order to maintain what traditional ascetical language calls the practice of virtue, which is the moderation of their instinctual desires. God has given us this limited freedom and expects us to use it, especially in entrusting the other forms of life and the planet itself to humans to take care of.

Teilhard de Chardin hypothesizes that biological evolution is virtually complete. The commandment in Genesis to increase and multiply and fill the earth has shifted to the spiritual plane and to higher levels of consciousness. The new thrust or focus of evolution is on human beings and their capacity for wholeness and union with God. The human family is at the threshold, both as individuals and as a species, of moving to a higher knowledge, understanding, and relationship with God. In other words, evolution has now opened us to stages of divine union and unconditional love.

The commandment is shifting its focus from "increasing and multiplying and filling the earth," not only with people, but with Divine Love itself.

This stage in human evolution puts the emphasis on higher states of faith and love and fosters the capacity to see God in everything and to respond to every situation according to God's will. This is where the Gospel of John comes into prominence with its spiritual perception of God's presence in all our senses, thinking, and especially, in our relationship to other people. This

26

spiritual perception is what interests those who feel called to personal transformation and union with God. This is a subject that is addressed in other world religions and in the Christian mystical tradition.

So here we are at the culmination of biological evolution and, while not trying to get along without it, we ask, what are we supposed to do now? What is the work of religions in the new situation or second axial period? Actually, we need this transformation in order to survive. We cannot prolong the battle of greed or domination with weapons of modern destruction without serious damage to ourselves and to all life on earth.

This situation means that living the spiritual life is the most important thing there is to do in the next stage in evolution. Living a spiritual life does not only lead to our salvation, healing, wholeness, and redemption. It involves the manifestation of the contemplative dimension of life, which is aimed at prayer and practice to further the capacity for transformation and to realize the New Creation that Jesus spoke about. The contemplative dimension of life has been a major part of the experience of those who have pioneered the new area of spiritual evolution.

It is possible to relate to God in almost any way you like, but because we have the experience of parents, we normally start off relating to God as father, mother, older brother or older sister, and then friend, companion, playmate, soul friend, spouse. Then we can move into the friendship and agapic love that conjugal love is to evolve into. There is the further possibility of serving God through humanitarian service or of dedicating one's life to God in a community of servant leadership.

Because of the interconnectedness of everything, we know that *relating* is what *being* really means. Just to be born is to be in relation with every other member of the human family, past, present, or to come, and with all creation. We depend on the other earlier levels of evolving creation for the necessary physiological tools to function on the human level. We are a microcosm in which all the expressions of creation are somehow present in each single consciousness, and it is capable of growth beyond anything that we can imagine. Jesus prayed "that they may be one even as we are one," suggesting a oneness and unity that is virtually unlimited.

How we relate to God then is an important issue no matter what our religion or even if we have no religion at all. People are sometimes so turned off by their religion that they have to leave it at least for a while in order to get over their anger towards some of the experiences they have been through. But that has to pass. Then the question, "What is a fully human being?"—or, more specifically, "Who am I?"—begins to emerge into prominent light.

One relationship that needs more attention today is our psycho-spiritual relationship with God.

Is God just dealing with us as a creature whose worship he is trying to obtain so that he can make us whole and save our soul? Or is God manifesting God's Self in us in a way that is unique, and which has the possibility of bringing the divine action into the human species in ways that have never been possible before, at least on the global scale?

29

Take for instance, the possibility of knowing God at ever deepening levels of consciousness. As Jesus suggested, "This is eternal life—to know the true God and Jesus Christ whom God has sent." This is not only conceptual knowledge. It involves our whole being—heart, mind, and body—working in a unified way to do God's will in each moment. In other words, it is possible to have a relationship to God in which God is acting in us more than we are. The discoveries of recent science have shown that the human species has a oneness that transcends all differences and that, in some way, we really are everybody else as well as ourselves. When we greet someone, we are greeting ourselves at the deepest level. Everybody has the Divine Presence in them and is saturated with God.

Teilhard de Chardin teaches that every sub-atomic particle is Christ. We are made up of trillions of them. So our very bodies are saturated with Christ all the time and he is manifesting in us. God is relating to us in everything that happens and in everyone we meet. To live in that world is a very different situation from

30

the world of competition and self-centered goals based on programs for happiness which are prompted by the instinctual needs for security, power/control, and affection/esteem.

The unity of the human race makes it possible for God to become human in such a way that in taking one person to himself, he takes everybody to himself and we become, if we consent, another incarnation of Christ—limited, of course—but united with Christ in so far as we consent to the invitation to divine union and transformation.

God is trying to bring us to a new and extraordinary place which Christ calls the New Creation. Getting there requires effort. Yet it is the place where we were originally created, according to the Book of Genesis— namely, the consciousness of being made in the image and likeness of God.

Fr. Carl: Is there any approach that would help a person clearly grasp the beauty of our basic goodness?

Fr. Thomas: The principal source of affirming our basic goodness is the knowledge that we are created in the image and likeness of God. Even if we are the worst of sinners, God is infinitely merciful and has identified with us in such a way that he has taken all our sins away.

The evolutionary perspective can help to heal the sense of our unworthiness and lack of trust in God. God expects us to have all kinds of faults since we are made out of absolute nothingness. It is going to take time for the faculties wounded by habits of sin to be physiologically and psychologically prepared to function in the purified organism.

That God wants us to be happy should be affirmed over and over again. The love of God is trying to make us equal in all possible respects to himself, at least from the psychological perspective: to enjoy the same freedom, the same peace, the same sense of well-being and security, the same love.

That is what God is asking us to accept. If we would do that, he will take care of all the rest.

So here we are emerging in the evolutionary process from the instincts, spontaneity, and irresponsibility of animal life into a self-reflective consciousness that operates with a vastly different set of values. It is meant to moderate the lower functions of living and encourage the transformation of each human organism, as a microcosm of all creation, into sharers of the divine life.

The Beloved, then, is trying to bring about the transformation of humans in accordance with their nature and that involves a certain freedom of choice. Through love, that human freedom can become more and more penetrated by divine freedom, self-surrender, trust, gratitude, and the other attributes of God that we can participate in. God says, "I want you to become God too, but this can only happen on my terms, which is to acknowledge that you are creatures made out of nothing. Once you accept that fact, you can have everything including me!"

The Christian contemplative perspective moves things more firmly in the direction of transformation than the natural state of humanity is capable of at its current level of evolution. The Gospel gives us a profound thrust toward divine union and eternal life. Evolution is not just moving us in the direction of deification, which the Greek Orthodox spiritual writers call divine union. Through grace, it awakens us to our participation in the divine life that is always present and available.

So does God love us? How much more evidence do you need!

THREE

Christ, Evolution and Religion

God is intimately present to each being ... ensures the subsistence and growth of each being, "continues the work of creation." The Spirit of God has filled the universe with possibilities and, therefore, from the very heart of things, something new can always emerge: Nature is nothing other than a certain kind of art, namely God's art, impressed upon things, whereby those things are moved to a determinate end. It is as if a shipbuilder were able to give timbers the wherewithal to move themselves to take the form of a ship.

—POPE FRANCIS, LAUDATO SI

The question has arisen whether we can be faithful to our own religion without loving the other religions that are trying to go in a similar direction.

Vatican II has given Catholics permission and encouraged them to acknowledge the work of the Spirit in other religions. This is an enormous breakthrough in religious attitudes. It does not mean that we are not wedded to our own religion. In our day the attitude toward missionary work has to be adjusted to emphasize collaboration and communion rather than conversion, because of the serious damage that often occurs. When religions get intertwined with politics resulting in religious wars, they discourage people from practicing any religion at all.

No one religion can contain the whole of God's wisdom, which is infinite. All religions have also embodied a certain amount of cultural conditioning. The work of Raimon Panikkar is especially useful in inter-spiritual dialogue. He bridges two great traditions, Hinduism and Christianity. He has studied their sources and sacred texts in great depth. In addition, he has had much exposure to Buddhism and other religious traditions. He looks at each religion and acknowledges what they have contributed, while also pointing out the cultural limitations of certain aspects of their teaching. The ultimate experience of God in this life is much more complex than we thought. We need the contributions of the spiritual traditions of all the religions, in order to enrich the basic core of wisdom of the human family itself.

If we do not do that, we set-off the defensive attitudes that led to violence in the past and are still leading to terrible violence, however much they are intertwined with political motives. We need to transcend each stage of the evolutionary process without ceasing to be rooted in our own tradition. All religions have truths that will lead to salvation. The question might be asked,

"Where has this idea of exclusivism actually led in the past?" It seems to have led to religious wars and to attitudes of defensiveness. The claim that "our religion is the only one leading to salvation"—a position long held by many Christian denominations—was laid to rest for Catholics by Vatican II.

There is a difference between being a member of the best religion and the one that suits us the best. Some will be attracted to a particular religion for a number of reasons that are not easily recognized. The Fathers at the Vatican Council certainly looked into this issue in great depth. They were inspired by outstanding figures like Cardinal Augustin Bea.

I was brought up to hold this exclusivist view, too. My grandma, who was a devout Episcopalian, and I were great friends. She had a special affection for me because I bore the name of her beloved husband. I remember at eight years old wondering whether she could be saved and whether she would ever get to heaven. This caused me no little anxiety because I loved her so much. When that belief was uprooted by the Vatican II decision, I was delighted. Grandma was obviously a lovely person, so the idea that she could not be saved just because she did not profess certain dogmas did not seem fair to me. According to Scripture, "God wills everyone to be saved." So I do not know on what scriptural basis people say that Christianity is the *only* true religion.

Maybe this kind of exclusivity was a necessary step in the religious evolution of human consciousness. Maybe people would not have practiced any religion at all unless they thought that theirs was the right one. This kind of tribalism appeals to something very deep in the human psyche. Security is one of the chief emotional programs for happiness, and in a matter of such importance as one's salvation, certitude about one's religion is about as much safety as you can hope to get in this world. How much of that certitude is coming from genuine faith, and how much from the psychological need of being right and the feeling that one is on the sure road to heaven? The affirmation of exclusivity tended to contradict the basic equality of humans in times past and that led not just to controversy, but to the worst kind of violence.

Religion offers the greatest security of all securities: "I'm in the right religion." Maybe you are in the right religion for you, but to insist that all those in other religions are going to be condemned and excluded from heaven, including those who never even heard of Christ in the centuries before his birth? God wants everybody to be saved, according to 1 Timothy.

Fr. Carl: What about Jesus Christ? We believe Jesus Christ is the Way, the Truth, and the Life.

To know Christ is a key to being saved. What are some of the new ways in which we look upon Jesus Christ as man and as the Son of God?

Fr. Thomas: We believe that Christ is fully God and fully human at the same time. As God, he is the Word of God that created humanity from the beginning; hence, he has been at work in the world since the first man and woman became fully human. Christ has brought his divine nature into the human species in such a way as to influence and enrich the human species backwards and forwards in time, as well as right now.

In God, time and space serve as his means of creating and allowing evolution to unfold. He has given time for things to unfold materially. It is going to take time for humans, both mentally and spiritually, to unfold and to understand what their developing consciousness perceives about God. If God is interested in saving the whole human race, as Scripture affirms, all the people who came before Christ could not possibly have known him as the man Jesus, but they could have had a direct relationship with him through the Word of God as Christ.

What Christ did in becoming human was to take every person into himself. The whole of human nature has been transformed by God becoming human. Everything in creation relates to the human presence of Christ in every human being, Christ emphasizes in the Gospel, "Whatever you do to the least of my little ones, you do to me." The Presence of Christ is emphasized not only in humanity in general but in each individual. For some of the mystics, the experience of this Presence is very strong.

Mother Teresa, for example, saw Christ in the most destitute of people.

Fr. Carl: So because Jesus Christ became one with all humanity, if I'm sitting here as a Hindu, I am benefiting from that Presence within me even though I am not aware of it.

Fr. Thomas: Karl Rahner proposed the idea that many people are anonymous Christians. Vatican II theology has gone even further in affirming that Christ is not only present in everybody, but is present in all the religions through their rituals and forms of teaching. In this sense, he is relating to them through their own practices as he relates to us as Christians through the Gospel and sacramental system.

The emerging Christ in evolution is gradually taking possession of all creation. Human nature summarizes each level of evolution up to the present time: that is, matter, plant life, animal life, hominids, and now human beings.

Fr. Carl: Has a Hindu ever said to you they resent the idea that you think they are being saved through Christ?

Fr. Thomas: Yes, they do in inter-religious dialogue. The exclusivity proclaimed by any religion turns them off. To say they are being saved through Christ is likely to be offensive, whereas to say that they can be saved through their particular religious practices might be acceptable. There needs to be an openness to dialogue among all the religions. Dialogue uncovers the common experiences of silence, prayer, worship, and service that go by different names in the various religions, but for most of them all of these are often present.

A Zen master once said to me, "If Christ has taken away the sins of the world, where are they?"

Good question. They are nowhere. They have been obliterated is one explanation. People project onto God the way they would act under certain circumstances. To think otherwise requires a lot of humility and sitting a little lightly on our doctrinal convictions. Following my conversion when I was 17, I was a strictly observant

Catholic. My devotion to the Church was about as thorough as you can get. I left behind my family and all its values, including their plans for me and all the things they thought or hoped I could do.

All I wanted at that time was to follow Christ. I had intended to be a lay brother because that was the lowest place. That was the call of the Gospel for me as I heard it. To come out of that very strict thinking has taken years. This is why I admire the patience and skill with which God gradually heals our excesses without undermining our self-acceptance in such a way that we give up all religion, as happens to some people. I have desperately tried to understand other religions in terms of the Christian religion. As time goes by, I feel more and more comfortable with seeing that doctrine is not the problem; it is the level of consciousness with which people interpret each other's doctrine. This can be very narrow and limiting, distorting its purpose.

As one's mind is clarified, one can see the spiritual meaning of scriptural texts, a meaning that was completely inaccessible when we relied on our rational judgment alone without the experience of prayer and interior silence. These practices relativize attachment to our convictions without taking them away. What is taken away is attachment to the certitude of being right. This is a liberating process that will continue to develop.

FOUR

Christ, Evolution and All Creation

The Divine calls us all into being out of itself.
We are meant for it: That is the point of the spiritual
journey. The journey puts us on the road to realizing and
actualizing who we really are in our ultimate being
... and awakening to and developing compassion,
sensitivity and love.

—WAYNE TEASDALE

When we read the statement in John's Gospel in which Jesus says, "No one comes to the Father except through me," we need to look at the full meaning of that statement. Obviously, many people existed before the man Jesus Christ entered history, so the statement does not seem quite consistent with other ideas that Scripture speaks of—for example, about God willing the salvation of all and sending Christ for the salvation of all. Here is a suggestion as to what the meaning of that statement might be.

We saw that according to Catholic doctrine and the Council of Chalcedon, Christ has two natures. That means that Christ has a fully human nature in every respect as well as a fully divine nature, specifically the nature of the Eternal Word of God. It is that Eternal Word that became flesh.

53

So the activities of this human being have to be appropriated to the Divine Word as his own.

The Father gives himself totally to the Son in the Trinitarian relationships—so much so, that God lives in the Son rather than in himself.

The Father in Trinitarian theology contains infinite possibilities. Or we could say that these infinite possibilities are emerging out of absolute nothingness into the Son, who actualizes all the possibilities within the Father, manifests them fully within the Trinity and expresses them by virtue of the Incarnation throughout all time and space.

The Word not only became flesh, but also created everything that exists and without whom nothing exists. The Father can only be found in the Son because that is where the Father lives. From this perspective, "No one comes to the Father except through me" is an obvious consequence of the relationship of the Father and Son within the Trinity. There is no place to find the Father except in the Son who is also the Word Made Flesh. The statement does not mean that other people are excluded. Christ as the Word has been working in the world from the beginning of time. Jesus speaks sometimes from his human nature and sometimes from his divine nature as the Son of God, especially in the Gospel of John. In the Gospel of John, Jesus's sayings are quite different from his sayings as they appear in the synoptic gospels. John's Gospel seems to reflect the contemplative experience and reflection on the meaning of Christ's life, Resurrection, and Ascension that the community of contemplatives has thought through over many years.

Fr. Carl: Would it be fair to say that Christ has been active from the beginning of time and that his activity was manifested in Jesus for just a period of time?

Fr. Thomas: Yes, but that period is continuing in time. There was a time when Christ did not exist in time. But the Word of God was creating everything that exists. So when we use the term "Christ," we are referring to the divine nature that possesses the humanity of Jesus that in John's Gospel is called the "Word" and in Paul's terminology is called the "Christ." Christ is the divine person who is functioning in the universe from the beginning of time and became flesh in time in the humanity of Jesus Christ.

Theologians speak of "high" and "low" Christology, referring to a Christology that emphasizes the divinity (high), and one that emphasizes his humanity (low). According to the Council Fathers of Chalcedon, Jesus is fully human and fully divine without any confusion of natures. This is a mystery in the sense that we cannot understand it by reason and rational consciousness alone.

Actually, the evolutionary view reveals Christ as intimately present in all humanity and humanity in him. Christ can thus draw people to salvation and to God through means other than their religion, and even outside of religion. For instance, there are other ways that God leads people to himself such as art, science, love of nature and the service of others. Sometimes, people who have no religion are more generous in seeking God and in helping other people than the people in it.

Christ's Incarnation represents an enormous thrust of the human family, now that he has made it his own, towards transformation and transcendence and to becoming God's original plan for creation, which is to share the divine life with everyone in so far as that is possible. He is manifesting the incredible humility of God which seems to desire not to be God. In doing so, Christ has given us an example of humility that can hardly be surpassed.

As Paul says in Philippians, Christ chose "Not to regard being equal with God something to cling to." If the living Word of God did not care about being God, what does that say about the pretentions of people who want to live and become God on their own terms? Jesus is the manifestation of the dispositions of the Trinity, which includes infinite compassion and self-giving.

In the formation of attitudes towards God, some psychological background is helpful. People write or talk from their cultural backgrounds without being aware of their own limitations, prejudices, and exaggerations. To know nothing is probably the safest way of avoiding the problem of dogmatism or doctrinal dependency when such a dependency is only part of the picture, however important. There has to be experience in order to adapt doctrinal teaching to the actual lifestyles of people, based on the example of humility that Christ has given us. He became the lowest of the low by taking the lowest place, gathering us to himself by identifying with the sins of the world, and taking the consequences of our sins into himself.

Perhaps we can say that God adjusts himself to each of the creatures whose nature he created. He gives himself entirely, but is limited by the particular nature that the creature has. When it comes to humans, we have a capacity to respond and to relate to values that are trans-sensible. God relates to us as persons because we are persons.

As Teilhard de Chardin says, God is present in every subatomic particle. The Divine Presence penetrates all that exists. Everything by virtue of coming into existence is in relationship to its Source. We emerge through the evolutionary process into a new kind of creature. This doctrine emphasizes once again the incredible closeness and openness with Christ that is not only possible, but is already the fact.

Fr. Carl: Is the doctrine you are talking about the Incarnation?

Fr. Thomas: The doctrine I am talking about is God's presence in everything that exists including, of course, the Incarnation. The Incarnation gives to all creation and to humans in particular an immense thrust towards transformation, not just into higher states of consciousness, but into God-consciousness in so far as we are capable of receiving it.

Fr. Carl: So in many ways, we have put Jesus Christ in a box, haven't we?

Fr. Thomas: I am afraid so, possibly by emphasizing his humanity unduly. He himself said to his disciples, "It is important for you that I go." It is important for most of us on the spiritual journey that at some point our relationship with Christ that may be sensibly consoling, mentally stimulating, and spiritually reassuring, be removed so that we can work directly with Christ as God. Christ, becoming man, did not come to us so that we could be devoted to him, but so that we would let him take us to the Father. As Paul said, it is through Christ that we have access to the Father.

We see in the Gospels that Christ sometimes speaks from his human nature and involvement in the multiplicity and diversity of life situations, and at other times, from his spiritual communion with the Father, for which his whole life was oriented. In other words, he came to manifest the Father, not himself, and he only taught what the Father had taught him. According to Paul, he deliberately became a slave and the servant of all. As Abbé Huvelin writes, "Christ has so taken the lowest place that no one can ever take it from him." The lowest place is the place of honor in the Kingdom of God.

As we progress in our spiritual journey, we may begin to feel the same inclinations as Jesus as we progress, so that we can see humiliation and suffering, not as self-diminutions or disasters, but as benefits. What life actually brings us, more than our own choices, is much more sanctifying and healing than any plans of ours. God's will is all embracing. He treats us with both humor and seriousness at the same time, because his project is to transform this tiny thinking animal into the spitting image of Christ in his humanity, which was totally possessed by the Word of God.

Mary was significant in the early church because she is the image of what Baptism is supposed to do, that is, to bring forth the Word of God in our personal humanity. It is an awesome prospect.

Since Christ has been glorified in his Ascension, he shares the divine attributes in an eminent way and can do the same things that the Divine Essence can do in regard to knowledge and power. As he said, "All power is given to me in heaven and on earth." He can live in us, and he prays that we will allow him to do so. All that is promised in Baptism is completely fulfilled in the Ascension, which is a statement that God's plan is to make us God, too. How much closer can you get to God than to be living in the bosom of the Father?

In the experience of silence, especially if it is deep, you may experience at times a certain pure awareness. Even if it is brief, you are in contact with That Which Is, and this Reality is obviously in love with you.

FIVE

—

Into Unity Consciousness

Forsake everything that is yours. Undertake this,
and let it cost you everything you can afford.
There you will find true peace, and nowhere else.

... Never think too much about what you could do, but
about what you could be. ... As we are holy and have being,
to that extent we make all works holy, be it eating, sleeping,
keeping vigil or whatever it may be... What matters is the
ground on which the works are built.

—MEISTER ECKHART

The awakening of the inner eye of faith is the awakening of the contemplative process. You begin to see the Divine Presence in everything without effort—even when the necessities of daily life require your full attention. When the inner eye of faith is thoroughly opened, it is a fairly permanent state of mind. You see everything as it is, but you also see it in its Source which is the presence of God. In the case of creatures like us with a certain free choice, you may encounter God in actual sense experiences. We are also meeting God in the presence of other people and events. The fruits of meditation are available in everyday life in the sense that one is always in the presence of God, even in very engaging and complex mental activities.

To see God in everything, however hidden, is an enormous enhancement of the capacity of perception. This kind of seeing is not, of course, like looking through a microscope, but involves perceiving the invisible Presence and Source of everything present in the smallest particles and beyond. God is always speaking to us not in our language, but in his language, which is silence. If God is trying to tell us something, a sentence or phrase may come up on an inner screen of consciousness, and you are given the whole sentence at once. You also may get what seems like a kind of subtle nudge, or hint. The message is there in a few words and usually clearer than at other times.

The Divine Presence is always within us. This Presence can be understood as the glorified Christ, the Holy Spirit, the Trinity, a brief encounter with higher consciousness, or with the Self. God has innumerable and surprising ways of communicating and they are all incredibly valuable. Some may become more extended at later stages of our journey.

The practice of silence allows God greater freedom to act in us as our interior life becomes freer from our predispositions and predetermined mindsets. That is why it is necessary, even in doctrinal loyalty, to sit lightly on the propositions in the literal sense, because time and further human evolution may change the meaning of certain words. They have already changed in the creed to such a degree that some people think the creed has to be redone because it gives impressions different from what theology has evolved to. In other words, by sitting lightly on the literal sense of theological propositions, you are open to better expressions of them as time goes on. These particular expressions do not, of course, contain the reality; they can only point to it. The purpose is to use them as guidelines to experience the mysteries of Christ.

Fr. Carl: You put a lot of faith in the moment of death, as I have listened to you talk through the years.

Fr. Thomas: Not only the moment of death, but the *process of dying*. Remember that the process has steps, so you have to expect significant changes of attitudes previously held. Death is a transformative process that can be reproduced in daily life by spiritual practice or with a guide who is well qualified.

God hides behind visual things in such a way that he is never absent. The person whose inner eye of faith has opened, perceives Divine Presence in a way that is intuitive. Then we hear things in a new way. We are always listening, no matter what is being said, to the sound of sheer silence, which is God's abiding communication. Between the syllables, between the words, or just by sitting still, we can come to deep listening. This is done in Lectio Divina by reading slowly and pausing when we feel drawn to silence. This is allowing silence to morph into Presence, a presence that is clearly God's Presence. When Divine Presence is felt, other ways of getting there become obsolete, at least for the moment.

The attraction to silence is like the attraction of the sense of smell in relation to pleasant odors. It is an attraction to something delightful. Silence, solitude, and contemplative prayer draw people inwardly. You could say that God is hiding behind and within the perfumes. I suppose incense and fragrant candles have the same purpose.

The experience of touch is the sensation of being kissed or embraced, held, or even cuddled. The Presence is then felt in a way that reveals that Presence to our bodies, minds, and spirits all at the same time.

Taste is the sense of God's presence arising from within us. Scripture speaks of sensing God like the taste of honey in the mouth. The *Song of Songs* provides an abundance of similar erotic images.

While these experiences are not the purpose of the spiritual journey, they are a kind of romantic aspect of it that is more important than some may think. There is certainly an erotic side to God.

That would suggest that there is a passion in God to communicate himself. He is not just passively interested in us. God is not only looking for us in a general sort of way, but is looking for us with immense energy and eagerness. Through the Prophet Isaiah, God affirmed that he desired Israel like a bridegroom on his wedding night. This is not a thought; it is an eagerness and passion to share oneself and to be loved in return.

On the night of the Resurrection, Christ visits the disciples in an upstairs room. He first says, "Peace be to you." And then he shows them his wounds. He repeats, "Peace be to you." Peace is like a divine kiss. It establishes a disposition of readiness for a relationship of communion with another person. And then he breathes on them. This is a very significant symbol that he goes on to clarify in case there is any doubt, saying: "Receive the Holy Spirit." The giving of the Spirit is the *interpenetration of spirits*. It is the consummation of the spiritual marriage that is described in Christian bridal mysticism. The spiritual marriage moves to ever deeper levels of selfless love and service of one another.

The continuing experience of loving God with fidelity, trust and self-surrender begins to move into unity consciousness in which God and us are not separate. This is not usually a permanent state because of the usual things we have to do to survive in this world. But it presupposes that after the transforming union, a new level of Christian life opens up to a further stage beyond union with God—even bridal union as wonderful as that is—to unity with God who takes over the faculties more and more completely and manifests himself in everything we do. The Spirit suggests what the right response to every situation is from the perspective of divine love. Jesus refers to that level of love when he speaks of the Eucharist, saying, "Those who eat me shall live because of me." Christ becomes the source of all our activities. There is no I, then there is no me. All self-interest is transformed into abandonment to the divine will and to manifesting that disposition in every situation.

In the no-self situation, there is only the doing what has to be done, without self-reflection.

This is non-duality, which is a focus of interest in inter-spiritual dialogue at the present time. This is heaven on earth. At the same time, it is extremely simple and ordinary. It does not need extraordinary consolations anymore, and still less, visions. It consists of leading ordinary life from this extraordinary perspective of allowing God to manifest in us rather than for us to act from ego and the false self. There is no more need of God hiding because we are growing in the physical capacity to handle more intense communications of divine life without being overwhelmed by the divine majesty or getting sick. Many mystics had a lot of sickness—that's because their bodies were not sufficiently prepared for the sublime graces they were receiving. God has to go slow in order not to overwhelm our weakness. In fact, weakness becomes our greatest treasure because this transformation into Christ comes about *only* from God and through his totally gratuitous generosity, not through anything we can do.

In the movement from the false self and ego into no-self and no-ego, God is taking over all our faculties and manifesting himself appropriately, even in our smallest actions and bodily necessities.

So, suppose you want to serve a meal or clean the house. It is not just you who are doing these things, but God. In other words, the "me" that tends to get stamped on every human experience is erased and replaced by a direct

72

communication with God in which he does all the doing and we do all the receiving.

Whatever you do is Christ living in you. You become another incarnation without, of course, the completeness that we believe, as Christians, occurred in Jesus Christ. This is something that grows in you as you keep doing meditation and practices to reduce the obstacles in both your conscious and unconscious awareness. There's no self but there is certainly some kind of identity because he created us. But, who wants to think of yourself if you have God's presence and action all the time?

We are dealing with God manifesting in diversity and in creation so that we can relate to him, so that we are an "I" that can be in relationship with the "Thou" of God. But when the I has become the Thou, then you are in a different situation. All the ways of perceiving God shift in that new light. The senses are translated into various presences of God, which are then translated into just doing what needs to be done without thinking about it, but knowing that it is coming from God. You are dealing with the un-manifest God, which

73

is, I presume, a greater participation in God's "is-ness" than in dealing with him as the Creator God, however exalted that invitation may be.

The actual spiritual life is about becoming nothing. Then you can become everything, which is what God is. If we are interested in self-gratification on the level of the unreal—the false self, the ego, or society's ideas of happiness—then God cannot adorn us with the riches of divine life. Letting what happens just happen, without thinking about it and without criticizing or judging it, but seeing it as something God is sending, is a characteristic disposition in most spiritual traditions, once a person reaches the freedom to let go of the self.

SIX

Playing with God

What is serious to men is often very trivial in the sight of
God. What in God might appear to us as "play" is perhaps
what he himself takes most seriously. ... If we could let go
of our own obsession with what we think is the meaning
of it all, we might be able to hear his call and follow him in
his mysterious, cosmic dance. ... We are invited to forget
ourselves on purpose, cast our awful solemnity to the winds
and join in the general dance.

—THOMAS MERTON

God in his essence does not need anything and does not have to create. What is he going to do? Maybe he might like to play games.

We might ask the question: Is the journey of this life and the evolutionary process that we are immersed in a serious and even desperate situation all the time? Maybe we take it too seriously. It is serious! Being created out of nothing is a humbling situation. It seems that God has created everything with a certain humor and even playfulness. In the *Book of Wisdom* we read that God delighted to be living with his human creatures and playing with them.

If this is true, what games does God like to play? Certainly "Hide and Seek" seems to be a favorite game of his. God hides and we keep seeking! Once in a while he tosses out some sign of his presence. We do not get the whole of God each time he acts in our lives because that would end the game.

While we are living in this world, God can only spoon-feed us, or even use a kind of eye-dropper, to give us just a little bit of himself at a time, because if he presented himself just as he is, we would disappear into the nothingness from which we came. At the very least, the light would be too bright and we would be blinded by it. In states of deep interior purification, when God does turn up the divine light, it is so bright that the soul experiences darkness rather than his Presence, according to Saint John of the Cross in *The Dark Night of The Soul*.

Besides "Hide and Seek," God seems to have other favorite games such as "Let's Pretend." Let's Pretend means....let's pretend that God is always close; or let's pretend that God is absent and far away; or let's pretend that God is in a deep relationship with us that we can feel. In the Christian scriptures when the text reads that God is angry, threatening, or about to punish us, might he be playing this game of pretending?

Another game is "Let's Do It Again." Think of the actions that God does over and over again like making stars, planets and galaxies. You might think he would get bored. Then he destroys them. There is a child-like aspect to the divine way of operating. Think of a little child that builds a set of blocks into a tower, knocks them all down, and then starts to build another tower saying, "Let's do it again! That was such fun!"

How human beings react to the same or different situations is often quite humorous. Humans get themselves into all kinds of trouble that God must sometimes find amusing. Our pretentions and presumptive attitudes can be so ridiculous.

In one retreat that I recall, the retreat master spoke of what it would be like if we could create a little clay person, who then started bawling us out for what we did or did not do. Having created it out of nothing, most of us would just knock this clay figure to smithereens. But God allows himself to be insulted, criticized, denied, even rejected. At the same time, the presumptuous character of this little clay man might strike him as funny. We can see a humorous side in Jesus too. Some of his parables or similes are laughable, like a camel going through the eye of a needle. Recall the way he frequently dealt with his disciples, taking their foibles into account and not blaming them for their faults, but inviting them to more mature ways of behavior.

Perhaps God also likes sports. Maybe basketball. If we would take the role of the basketball, it could be quite an exciting game. For instance, the harder a basketball hits the floor, the higher it rises. So, if you hope to rise really high, you have to expect there is going to be a huge bump to begin with. The best shot in a basketball game is for it to hit the floor so hard that that it bounces into the basket. Sometimes God is a player in the game and sometimes he is the referee and keeps score. He usually does not let us in on just what the score is or our contribution to it. Maybe the game has no score or maybe he does not care. To have fun is the chief reason to take part in any game.

Another aspect of a basketball game is the action of dribbling. If you want to get to the basket from the opposite end of the court, you are required to bounce the ball all the way, or the referee blows his whistle. As the ball, you keep hitting the floor—bang, bang, bang! This is often our experience in the spiritual journey—one difficulty

82

after another. The blows come fast and furious and we have not yet reached the basket. The game can also get a little rough. The opposing players may try to drag the ball out of our hands or bump us out of their way.

Perhaps some games are designed by God to see how far we will go. In other words, when do you say "enough?" Are you going to call for a timeout? Meanwhile, God is seeing whether we want to learn how to play these games. And if we are too stuffy or staid, he may choose games that are more in line with our tastes, because otherwise we might not play at all.

Suppose, however, we decide to be like Saint Thérèse of Lisieux when she described herself as a little ball that God can play with or throw into a corner and forget about. She recommends trying to *capture* God with little sacrifices. A game would fit that category nicely. She came to think of herself as a little ball in the hands of Jesus that he could bounce around or put on the shelf in the closet. In other words, he can do with her whatever he wants. She gives us an image of complete collaboration with whatever the games might turn out to be, including the rough ones. Father Jean-Pierre de Caussade calls this "abandonment to divine providence."

Obviously, God is careful not to play too rough. Otherwise we might become sick or injured. The game is normally adapted to each one's capacity and understanding. In any case, we need to try to realize that there is a playful side to the Creator and to the spiritual journey. It would be wise not to think of the spiritual journey as always serious, or so serious that we can never smile, relax, or challenge God by certain games that we might want to introduce into the game.

To stomp off the playing field or the basketball court and sit down in a huff is not the way to react. So, we might ask our self: Is this situation really so serious? Or just a little game? Or is God just looking to see if I am willing to play a little more vigorously today than I did yesterday?

When we look at the possibilities of embracing this insight, we see that we can relate to God in an intimate and close partnership while at the same time depending on and trusting God in everything we do. It would lead to a marvelous psychological, spiritual, and realistic kind of interaction. Perhaps the sense of God's playfulness would also help us to realize that the spiritual journey is mostly God's work. We do not have to conform to some particular pattern of discipline, but can choose whatever is most effective for our needs, as far as we can recognize them. The rest is up to God and his love for us.

Practices for daily life and prayer will continue to change as our relationship with God deepens and we learn more about how he functions. In time, we can see God in a new role as psychiatrist or psychoanalyst. We realize that he knows us through and through, along with all the obstacles we place to our spiritual progress. This psychological relationship with God enables him to lead us ever so wisely, but ever so gently.

The spiritual journey, of course, is not just a game. It is a game *plan*. It gives God a chance to reveal his willingness to take risks, his love of surprises, and his desire to further our human and spiritual development. Nature is very slow-moving, so we have to take that into account as well.

Sometimes you cannot figure out what the purpose of the game is—you just have to play and hope for the best. And we cannot expect to know what the result is, or whether we are winning or losing. Sometimes we can feel that we cannot handle a particular game. It then does not seem like a game anymore but a terrible burden. The goodness of God, however, is never questionable. When we start wanting to win the game, that is the end of the game, which is meant to be fun.

As soon as you make a career out of it, you have got something else going. And indeed, that seems to happen in professional sports of all kinds.

The normal purpose of a game is to have fun. Once you have a specific objective like winning, you turn the game into a work project. Winning is not the purpose of ordinary games. It is our particular mindset in our sports-saturated culture, where sport is becoming the primary religion of almost everybody. People even pray to win, which is to miss the point of playing at all.

In the spiritual world you do not know whether you are winning or losing most of the time, because who is

86

to judge? Every game has its own rules. God sometimes is the referee, but most of the time, he plays in the game too. He has the freedom to do anything. Or, not to do anything... So, let's play!

SEVEN

Silence and Centering Prayer

Contemplative prayer is a process of interior
transformation. ... One's way of seeing reality
changes. ... A restructuring of consciousness takes
place which empowers one to perceive, relate and respond to everyday life with increasing sensitivity
to the divine presence in, through and beyond
everything that happens.

—THOMAS KEATING

Fr. Carl: Can Centering Prayer take us all the way to divine union, Thomas?

Fr. Thomas: That depends on how you understand Centering Prayer. Yes, if you understand it not just as a practice, but as a stepping stone to divine union in the Christian contemplative tradition. One must also obey the insights or the inspirations of the Spirit that emerge through a regular practice of Centering Prayer, which then expands into ordinary daily life through attentiveness to the presence of God in all our activities.

Centering Prayer reduces the obstacles and releases the positive energies of the spiritual organism of sanctifying grace that is hidden from us in what might be called the ontological unconscious. Psychological memories in the unconscious may remain in the body and we may be under their influence without our being aware of it.

Our nervous system frequently responds with negative feelings that are inappropriate for the circumstances of the present and proves that we are being influenced secretly by the pain that was so bad that we repressed it into the psychological unconscious, where often it is unknown to us.

Our sensitivity to the inspirations of the Holy Spirit within us is crucial. If we pay attention to them, the positive resources of grace that have been buried in our unconscious up to now begin to activate. Our effort consists in reducing the obstacles, not in cultivating the resources of grace, because these resources are gifts. You cannot turn wisdom on, and you cannot endure the results of the Gift of Understanding unless you have been prepared by the earlier beatitudes. What is happening is that all the values of human nature are being enormously enhanced by Christian principles that are expressed in the practice of virtue, prayer, self-surrender, and above all, in recognizing and accepting our nothingness. The only thing our Blessed Mother claims in the Magnificat as interesting God is her nothingness. Her surrender is not built on anything else. "He has looked with kindness on my nothingness," she says in the Magnificat.

Nothingness refers to our creation. We emerged from nothingness and can do nothing of ourselves that has any relationship to deification or transformation. Most cultural belief systems are congenial to our emotional programs for happiness, but from the point-of-view of reality, are a lot of baloney! To feel, acknowledge, and consent to our creaturehood and to turn our life over completely to God, is the fundamental principle of true religion. A balance between our nothingness on one hand and confidence in God's presence, love, and support at the same time needs to be preserved throughout the journey.

Paul expresses this breadth of view in describing one of his transforming experiences of ecstasy. He says he was drawn up into the third heaven and heard things he could not repeat. When he comes back to Earth and to ordinary earthly life, he is hit by a "thorn of the flesh" that he recognizes as sent by God. He does not say what it is. He prays to God three times for healing. Three in Scripture usually means with great intensity or as much as possible. He prays ardently to be delivered because he thinks it might be interfering with his ministry, and it was. God's reply to his urgent petitions is interesting: "No, I'm not going to take this away. My power is made perfect in your weakness."

God is more concerned about Paul's humility and the acceptance of his weakness than about his ministry. Perhaps God is worried that Paul's spiritual exultation will interfere with the growth of his humility. Our transformation in Christ is God's primary purpose in all his gifts, because the greatest contribution we can make to God's glory and to his self-giving love for us is to give ourselves to God completely just as we are with all our failures, acts of injustice, and sins.

Humility is the great work of transmitting the Gospel rather than Paul's vocation as teacher of the Gentiles. God can raise up somebody else if we fail, but he cannot force the human will to accept its nothingness. That has to be a free choice. It is the fundamental condition for the growth of everything else. This is not because God is arbitrary or wants to be in control of the situation—it is because he is in control! That is reality.

Humility is the truth, and consenting to it, we are invited to give up the false self, the ego, and the separate-self sense, in exchange for enjoying the fullness of the Godhead. That's not a bad deal!

Abandonment to God's will is the main issue. It is crucial. You cannot do it without recognizing your nothingness as a creature. At the same time, it is using our experience of weakness, powerlessness, even sinfulness, to recognize God's humility and pure love for us in instituting a personal relationship with us by calling us out of nothingness into human consciousness.

Consciousness has evolved over time through the evolutionary process. From the beginning of time, grace has been available to people who have been introduced in some way to God's desire to have a relationship with them.

But I do not know whether you will discover the ontological unconscious without a discipline of silence and listening—deep listening. Lectio Divina is meant to lead to deep listening. Silence is perhaps the best access to God's presence within us. Listen and silence also so close to God that they are almost psychologically indistinguishable. That is why, as contemplative prayer develops, the less you do, the more God does. You cannot explain that to other people. They have to experience it. But you can urge them to do the practice. "Just do it!" And do it every day. And when you feel attracted, you might do it a little longer.

Interior silence morphs into the presence of God. Then silence is not just silence, emptiness, or nothingness. It is rather the best preparation for divine union there is, because over time it reduces all the obstacles. God's love is like the atmosphere that fills every empty space. I think that certainly, for much of my life and for most people's lives, it does not cross our minds how close a relationship God has with us and wants to enhance. That is why I keep mentioning the scientific evidence as a way of jogging people out of their bias against God's closeness or care for them. We do not like God interfering with certain attachments in our private lives.

A long life is meant to detach us from everything else we might do so that we finally agree to let God take over our lives more and more completely.

Centering Prayer is a process of liberation from the negative psychological damage of early childhood warehoused in the body. Whatever practice you might choose to reduce these obstacles is essential because they are like a straitjacket that prevents the positive energies of the Divine Presence within us to unfold. We have those powers, but we do not know what they are or how to use them without a regular practice of a discipline that reduces the obstacles and fosters the exercise of the Fruits and Gifts of the Spirit. We have those fruits within us from the moment of our conversion. We just don't know how deeply buried they are.

Silence allows both the movement of purification and of empowerment to take place at the same time. In a particular period of Centering Prayer, one is likely to predominate over the other. But as soon as you reduce any obstacle to the free flow of the grace of the Holy Spirit and its inspirations within you, you will begin to experience the Fruits and Gifts of the Spirit. These are liberating and heal the wounds of a lifetime, as well as our relationships with other people, including the most difficult ones.

The main thing that is necessary in the beginning of our spiritual life is to meditate every day to balance the activities of our day. If you do not have a daily contemplative practice, your activities, however well motivated, will wear you out over time, and you will suffer from burn-out or get discouraged and say, "This is more than I can do." God is never asking us to do more than we can do. To work hard and to give unceasingly is one thing, but to overvalue or over-believe in the things that we do when we really do not have the inner resources to sustain them is a lack of common sense and mature spiritual experience. By daily practice we further the values of the Gospel and the contemplative dimension of life in such a way that we promptly perceive and acknowledge our faults and renew and reaffirm our motivation over and over again to do all for God's love.

We live 24 hours a day. If we are living in a world of self-centered activities and by values that are not those of the Gospel, then the remembrance of God's special graces is hidden, especially the value of silence. We can give lip service to those values while, in fact, the more over-extended or exteriorized we are, the harder it is to return to deep silence. We might think "maybe tomorrow, or when I make my yearly retreat." The time for conversion and responding to God is always *now*, in this present moment.

So, it is important to have Centering Prayer as a stable habit, no matter what happens. You can kneel or lie down—the position doesn't matter.

Some positions are simply more conducive for prayer than others. The essence of contemplative practice is to open to the ever-present presence of God in interior silence. Then, whatever other practices you add to extend this disposition into daily life is up to you. To help us sustain our practice, a spiritual companion or friend is very helpful. I do not say a spiritual director, since you cannot always find one, or if you do, they may not have the right personality and spiritual experience for you. To have someone to share our struggles, remind us of the resolutions that we have made, and warn us when we are overdoing or underdoing something, is an enormous help.

EIGHT

Surrendering to Love

Every act of complete self-giving in the name of the fullness, even though you feel like you are isolated, ignored, unconnected, and meaningless, connects you immediately and becomes a sacrament of the manifestation of that dance of perichoresis, the fullness of love.

That's what happened in Jesus' case, that's what he is teaching. ... give yourself fully, hold nothing back because in this act of complete self-giving you make manifest what the kingdom of love looks like.

—CYNTHIA BOURGEAULT

Fr. Carl: Thomas, how has Centering Prayer deepened your awareness of the love of God?

Fr. Thomas: I was converted to pursue contemplative prayer when I was 17, during my first year at Yale University. I was reading books about contemplative prayer. Centering Prayer, as a term, did not exist yet. Whatever progress I made was based on pursuing the traditional teachings about meditation, especially Lectio Divina, not as separate methods, but as leading to resting in God—that is to say, moving beyond words and thoughts about words and feelings and, from time to time, to rest in God. Such is my understanding of what Lectio Divina is supposed to be. It is not spiritual reading. It is a specific way of reading Scripture that leads into interior silence so that the other acts of the Lectio Divina practice—how much you read, how much you reflect on the text, how much you express your aspirations in words—become briefer and the silence of all thoughts can be more frequent.

The whole thrust of Centering Prayer is to further the movement into resting in God in interior silence, which brings to an end our endless interior dialogue. This movement involves all the faculties, but in a more focused way than discursive meditation and reflecting on what one is reading. It is using our human faculties to move beyond them. Once you have moved beyond them, the movement towards silence becomes the primary focus of Centering Prayer. I had been doing this practice from 17 to about 45. We did not even think of Centering Prayer as such. The practice did not have a name. When the idea of trying to put the Christian contemplative tradition into a method arose—challenged by the excellent methods that Eastern spiritual teachers were providing in the West after World War II, which young people were certainly benefiting from—the whole thrust of Centering Prayer developed to offer a method to do what I just described.

To move through the stages of Lectio Divina as a method into its purpose, and where it takes you if you keep doing it, is a more direct, silent, and peaceful form of worship which is predominantly just the awareness of the presence of God. That is a movement that takes place in all spiritual practices. In Christianity, for example, you may be chanting the Psalms for a while without thinking of what the Psalms are saying. You are thinking of the Divine Presence to which you are addressing them.

Centering Prayer is not a term the founders created. It was suggested by a group of retreatants who were exposed to the whole process that I had been doing for 20 years. I had established the context for this prayer by developing the method and teaching the background, all of which went into the equation.

When you ask me how did Centering Prayer help me personally: It focused me more clearly on the goal I had been pursuing in my practice of Lectio Divina and brought about its final stage of resting in God and contemplative prayer.

There is a difference, of course, in Centering Prayer. It is directly focused on interior silence without the preliminary steps that occur in Lectio Divina. Resting in silence emerges directly in Centering Prayer, whereas

Lectio is based on the refining of words or phrases from Scripture and slips into this Presence, rather than continuing to reflect and make acts of the will. If, for instance, you are thinking of some event in Jesus's life, you do not follow those steps in Centering Prayer.

It is presupposed that you are doing Lectio at another time or have a stable practice of it that you developed earlier in your spiritual life. Centering Prayer is about silence and nothing else.

Lectio Divina can be done even if it is only about a single word. The word "Help," for example, can be Lectio Divina. We think of Lectio as reading a sacred text. The term "Lectio" is the movement into silence in which the reading from a Scripture text can be very brief. It can be an extended scriptural passage, but usually not a lot of reading because then you find you have too many thoughts for quiet prayer. It is a process that is focused on moving from its expression to its Source, and to the presence of God that rests in the depths of our being waiting to be discovered by us.

Centering Prayer that is reduced to a method is not really Centering Prayer. Centering Prayer as a movement into the dimension of contemplative prayer is a reflection on the mysteries of faith that have been digested and expressed in particular acts of affective prayer until it has simplified into a movement of the will that has become quasi-permanent, a way of letting go of the managing mind and transferring it to the heart, so that with practice, prayer becomes more "heartfulness" than "mindfulness."

Centering Prayer has to be taught with a certain expansiveness. It includes every effort at interior silence that evokes more and more of our total surrender to Divine Presence. As consent becomes more complete, our prayer is more a question of surrender and trust. You could call it just "surrendering to love," if you prefer. I find "love" an ambiguous word because it has so many different meanings in the English language, but is still the only one we have in English and we can give it the meaning we want.

Fr. Carl: What would you like to say to the community that you are part of?

Fr. Thomas: I can only recommend what the elders in monasteries have always said, which is, "persevere," meaning keep doing it—rain or shine. Since meditation is not only pleasant, but also purifying, do not be surprised by the ups and downs of your subjective experience and just accept what happens. This is when you truly consent in practice. You are giving away any control whatsoever over the results of what you are doing. It is allowing that consent to be purified by the Spirit, who will send into your life inwardly and outwardly the people, teaching, or trials that you need. The bottom line to that teaching is to place all our trust in God and in his determination to bring this about because of his immense, gratuitous love for us.

Fr. Carl: If you had 20 more years of life and prayer and study, what would you like to explore?

Fr. Thomas: What I am interested in now is surrender to the movement of letting go not only of the false self, but of self-identity, in the sense of being concerned about the work I have done or the work I might do. In other words, I am at the point where I do not want to do anything except God's will, and that may be nothing. But nothing is one of the greatest activities there is. It also takes a surprising amount of time! What time is left each day is an opportunity for God to take over my life more completely on every level and in every detail.

In a sense, it is a "no-I" and "no me" kind of project. By God's grace, I do not hang on to anything I have done. I appreciate all the people I have worked with, but now they are in God's hands. The work itself is really not my work; I was just trying to contribute something to the renewal of the Christian contemplative tradition by making it better known and available as a meditative practice. If it has gone farther than I expected, that is not my work but the Spirit that has moved it along and, hopefully, will move it farther in the theological vision of the future. I accept all at this point with a certain amount of lightness of touch that I can integrate new things.

In my understanding, the substance of it is that God is trying more and more to move the human race to the next stage of human consciousness, which is the capacity to respond to intuitive insights rather than rely as

109

heavily as we do on a rational, technological, and dominating kind of worldview. Such a perspective thinks of the human family as completely in charge of the rest of the universe and misses the reality of the equality of all creatures, especially human beings.

The truth is there is ultimately only one Self and this is God manifesting in us. God manifests most effectively when we are not thinking about ourselves at all. It is just being who you are as a human being and rational animal that is being deified in communion with all other human beings. We are influencing other people by personal spiritual work on ourselves, not for our own sake, but for the sake of the transformation in Christ of the whole human family.

I am absolutely certain that anyone in any religion or no religion who sincerely commits to the transformative process is changing the world more than they could by any other activity. In due time, they will have particular activities recommended to them by the Spirit as part of their vocation, but the most important work is to work on ourselves. We do not and cannot fix anybody else.

We cannot even fix ourselves. We become more and more certain of this through the experience of prayer, in our weakness, deprivations, the absences of God, and in daily life by our failures and humiliations.

All of these things are treasures planned by God with great love, not all at once—because we might be blown away—but to bear the trials of life as stepping stones in this transformative process by deepening our surrender. You do not really let go of anything when you accept and do God's will, because he never takes anything away from us except to provide something better or to incorporate us into a project that is better.

Moreover, we cannot do it alone. Without the encouragement and support of others, we might not rise to the generosity that is required to overcome our negative attitudes and situations.

Out of the maelstrom of activity—trials, suffering, and death—we experience resurrection. Any time the false self gives up something, it is death to something that was meaningful to us. The only thing that truly dies is the false self, the ego and the separate-self sense. Resurrection occurs in this life when we have significant breakthroughs from our dependency on the false self with its habitual misbehaviors and lack of understanding.

Fr. Carl: Of all the things that you have taught, what do you think is the greatest contribution you have made to help all of us understand more the contemplative dimension of the Gospel?

Fr. Thomas: My ideas, like everything else in my life, have changed and keep changing.

One's vision improves as the spiritual journey expands and deepens. I do not know what to say to your question because I do not feel that I have contributed anything.

I pray that I do not lead anybody astray or injure their faith in some way. But I think we have to stretch our understanding of certain religious terminology to include the vision that mystics and those advancing in the stages of consciousness perceive spontaneously, as they become liberated from the narrowness of attachment to sense experience and thinking—not that these are not good—but they are never the whole story.

The Divine Presence is happening in, through, and in the midst of every detail of life, so it should never be left out. I think this is what is meant in Scripture by living in the house of God. The house of God is all creation.

FATHER THOMAS KEATING (1923–2018)

Father Thomas Keating was a Trappist monk, priest, and one of the principal architects of the Centering Prayer movement, which revitalized the Christian contemplative tradition for contemporary seekers. Born in New York City in 1923, Keating pursued studies at Yale University and Fordham University before entering the Cistercian Order in 1944. He was ordained a priest in 1949.

In the 1970s, while serving as abbot of St. Joseph's Abbey in Spencer, Massachusetts, Keating, alongside fellow monks Fathers William Meninger and Basil Pennington, developed Centering Prayer—a method inspired by the 14th-century spiritual classic *The Cloud of Unknowing*. This practice emphasizes silent, wordless prayer as a means of consenting to God's presence and action within.

To support and disseminate this contemplative practice, Keating co-founded Contemplative Outreach in 1984, an international organization dedicated to teaching Centering Prayer and fostering spiritual growth. A prolific author, Keating's works include *Open Mind, Open Heart, Invitation to Love,* and *The Human Condition,* among others. His teachings continue to guide individuals seeking a deeper relationship with the Divine through the path of contemplative silence.

Wayfarer

PRESS & MAGAZINE

At Wayfarer Books we believe poetry is the language of the earth.
We believe words, like rivers through wild places, can change the
shape of the world. We publish poets and writers and renegades
who stand outside of mainstream culture; poets, essayists, and
storytellers whose work might withstand the scrutiny of crows and
coyotes, those who are cryptic and floral, the crepuscular, and the
queer-at-heart. We are more than just a publisher but a community
of writers. Our mission is to produce books that can serve as a
compass and map to all wayfarers through wild terrain.

WAYFARERBOOKS.ORG

SUPPORTING INDIGENOUS FUTURES
1% GIVEN BACK

Wayfarer Books is based in the San Juan Mountains near Mesa Verde, on the lands of the Ancestral Pueblo, the Southern Ute, the Weenuche (Mountain Ute), the Diné (Navajo), and the San Juan Southern Paiute Tribe. We honor the generations of Indigenous communities who have stewarded these lands for thousands of years. We acknowledge that this place was taken through genocide, colonization, and displacement. We respect the Indigenous peoples who remain here, both past and present. As one concrete act of accountability, we are launching 1% Given Back. Beginning in 2026, we will give 1% of Wayfarer's net profits directly to the Indigenous nations on whose lands we are based, in support of sovereignty, Indigenous futures, and wealth redistribution. We do this in the belief that acknowledgment should move beyond words and into tangible practice.

LEARN MORE AT WAYFARERBOOKS.ORG

www.ingramcontent.com/pod-product-compliance
Lightning Source LLC
Chambersburg PA
CBHW071156120626
46546CB00006B/2284